T0028772

To the scientists of the future —L.H.

For Embla & Elisa —X.L.

STEPHEN HAWKING

YOU
AND THE
UNIVERSE

WITH **LUCY HAWKING**

ILLUSTRATED BY **XIN LI**

Random House 🏠 New York

Although I cannot move and I have to speak through a computer, in my mind I am free.

I have spent my life traveling
across the universe inside my mind.

I have tried to answer some really big questions.

What's inside a black hole?

How big is the universe?

How many stars are there?

Is time travel possible?

But there are other big questions
I need *you* to help answer.

How can we take
care of each other?

How can we take
care of the planet?

How can we make the future
a place we want to be?

Every one of us, at every age,
can think about these questions
and come up with answers.

When we see the earth from space,
we see it's home to all of us.

One planet. One big family.

We are here together.

We can learn to live together
with kindness and respect.

I have been lucky in my work to help people
understand the universe.

But it would be an empty universe if it were not
for the people we love and the people who love us.

We are all time travelers,
journeying together into the future.

Be brave.
Be determined.
Let's work together to make that
future a place we want to visit.

And whenever you don't know what to do,
remember to look up at the stars
and not down at your feet.

QUESTIONS AND ANSWERS

What Is Inside a Black Hole?

Black holes are born from very large stars. Starlight comes from nuclear fusion. As stars burn, they create new material called elements. These include the oxygen we breathe, the calcium in your teeth, and even the precious metal gold. When a very large star burns up all its fuel, it creates a great big explosion called a supernova. This explosion sends the outer layers of the star, including the elements it created, out across the universe in a great big cloud of hot gas and dust. You, me, your family and friends, and all life on Earth are made of stardust.

After the star explodes, its inner core is left behind. If the star is really huge, at least twice the size of our sun, then the core can collapse in on itself and create a black hole! Black holes are so powerful, they drag in all the bits and pieces of everything that is unlucky enough to come close. This could include ripped-up pieces of stars, planets, and all kinds of space junk. Black holes are so far away that no one has ever visited one, although scientists have now taken a beautiful photo of a black hole. Maybe one day, we'll be able to peek inside!

How Many Stars Are There?

If it's a clear, dark night and you are far from any light, you can see so many stars, it's hard to keep track. Scientists who study stars are called astronomers. They use telescopes—some on Earth, some in space—that can see for huge distances. And they have powerful computers, which work with the telescopes to make maps of the sky. Using these tools, astronomers have been able to tell us there are around one hundred billion stars in our galaxy, the Milky Way. In the whole of the universe, there could be as many as one billion trillion stars. You'd need a lot of fingers to count all those stars!

How Big Is the Universe?

The quick answer is . . . it's enormous! Let's start close to home. The moon is 235,000 miles away from Earth. It takes around three days to get there, traveling in a spaceship. Our solar system is made up of Earth's neighbors, the family of planets and objects that, like Earth, rotate around our sun. The nearest planet to Earth in our solar system is Mars. But it's still really far away. A journey in a spaceship to Mars would likely take astronauts around nine months.

But if we zoom out of the solar system and travel out into the Milky Way, then we start to get an idea of how big the universe really is. If we were to voyage across the whole of the Milky Way, in a super-speedy spaceship traveling at the speed of light, it would take us 150,000 years!

And the Milky Way is only one of billions of galaxies in the universe!

This means the universe has to be super-duper huge to have space for all these galaxies with their stars, planets, black holes, and asteroids. We can only see a piece of the universe through our telescopes, and we call that the observable universe. It is ninety-three billion light-years across (meaning it would take light ninety-three billion years to go from one side of the observable universe to another).

We might not ever get to visit that far away or ever get to know what goes on in the far reaches of the universe. As far as we humans know, the universe is infinite, which means that it goes on and on and on and is bigger than we could ever possibly know.

Is Time Travel Possible?

If you could travel back in time, when and where would you want to go? Would you travel back millions of years to see the dinosaurs? Or perhaps you'd like to see what Planet Earth looked like to the first humans who looked up at the stars?

The light from the sun and other stars is coming to us from such a long distance away that it arrives following a time delay. So when we see the light of a star, we could be looking at a star that may no longer exist. In fact, every time we look at the sun, we see it not as it is at this very moment, but as it was eight minutes ago!

What about traveling into the future? Well, we do that every day. Every moment, we are living in what *was* the future and is *now* the present! That's why it's so important that we work together to make the future a place we want to visit—because it's somewhere that we are all going to go.

Do Aliens Exist?

We use the word "alien" to describe a life-form that lives on another planet and is different from the living creatures we already know. Nobody knows for sure whether they exist, but scientists are looking for them. Using radio telescopes, astronomers "listen" to the sounds of the universe to see if they can pick up a signal that indicates the existence of other forms of life. But scientists don't just listen—they also send out messages into space to see if anyone is listening to us!

So far, we haven't had an answer. But that doesn't mean aliens don't exist. It might be that other forms of life exist and they're just too far away from us to be able to make contact. Or maybe they have reached out and left us a message we can't read yet.

What do you see when you look up at the stars? Do you think other life-forms are out there? What do you imagine they look like?

ABOUT STEPHEN HAWKING
AND THIS EARTH DAY MESSAGE

Stephen Hawking was one of the greatest scientists of all time, and his work continues to have a big impact today! He spent his career making important discoveries about the nature of black holes and how the universe began. Stephen wanted everyone to understand what his work, and his fellow scientists' work, meant. So he spent a lot of time thinking of simple ways to explain complex science to make it interesting and accessible to as many people as possible.

Stephen wanted to leave a legacy for the scientists of the future. Toward the end of his life, he wrote a statement about the importance of science and technology, our shared future as humans on this planet, and the extraordinary ability of humans to solve big challenges. This

statement was broadcast as an Earth Day message by the European Space Agency and transmitted from a radio telescope toward a black hole to celebrate Stephen's life and achievements.

It's a simple message—with a very deep meaning. And this book is a version of that message. Stephen wanted his words to reach a wide-ranging audience—people of all ages, across all continents.

You and the Universe is intended especially for the very youngest scientists, those kids who are curious about the world and the cosmos. Above all, Stephen believed that science should be fun, engaging, and inclusive. Through *You and the Universe,* his mission of educating the youngest inhabitants of the planet lives on.